Get Motoring!
Buses

by Dalton Rains

FOCUS READERS® SCOUT

www.focusreaders.com

Copyright © 2024 by Focus Readers®, Mendota Heights, MN 55120. All rights reserved. No part of this book may be reproduced or utilized in any form or by any means without written permission from the publisher.

Focus Readers is distributed by North Star Editions:
sales@northstareditions.com | 888-417-0195

Produced for Focus Readers by Red Line Editorial.

Photographs ©: Shutterstock Images, cover, 1, 4, 7 (top), 7 (bottom), 9, 11, 13, 15 (top), 15 (bottom), 16 (top left), 16 (top right), 16 (bottom left), 16 (bottom right)

Library of Congress Cataloging-in-Publication Data
Names: Rains, Dalton, author.
Title: Buses / by Dalton Rains.
Description: Mendota Heights, MN : Focus Readers, [2024] | Series: Get motoring! | Includes bibliographical references and index. | Audience: Grades K-1
Identifiers: LCCN 2023031102 (print) | LCCN 2023031103 (ebook) | ISBN 9798889980070 (hardcover) | ISBN 9798889980506 (paperback) | ISBN 9798889981350 (pdf) | ISBN 9798889980933 (ebook)
Subjects: LCSH: Buses--Juvenile literature.
Classification: LCC TL232 .R35 2024 (print) | LCC TL232 (ebook) | DDC 629.222/33--dc23/eng/20230706
LC record available at https://lccn.loc.gov/2023031102
LC ebook record available at https://lccn.loc.gov/2023031103

Printed in the United States of America
Mankato, MN
012024

About the Author

Dalton Rains is a writer and editor who lives in Minnesota.

Table of Contents

Buses 5

Parts 8

Uses 12

Glossary 16

Index 16

Buses

Buses drive on roads.

They carry many people.

People ride buses to go places.

Some buses drive in the city.

Other buses drive long distances.

Parts

A bus has doors. It also has wheels and **headlights**.

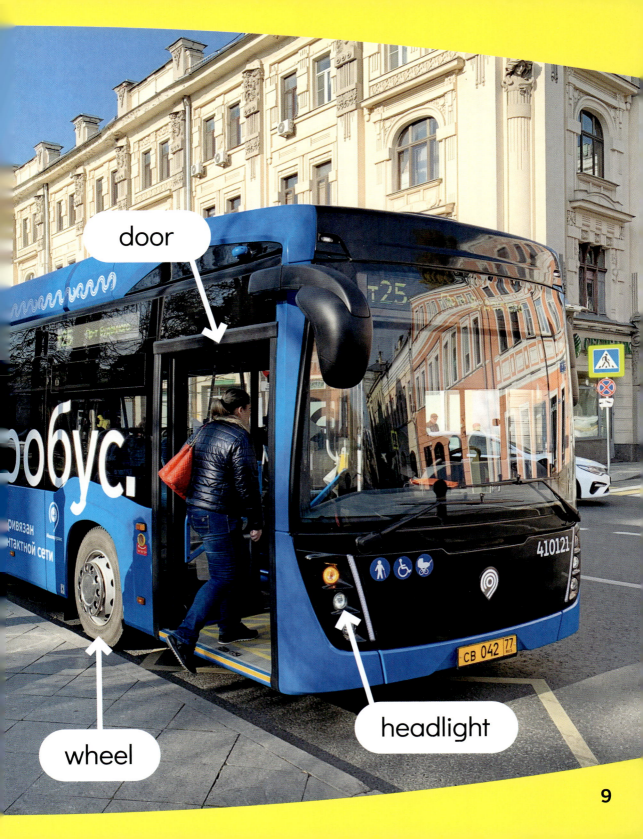

Inside, there are many seats. People can look out the windows while they ride.

Uses

Each bus has a **route**.

The bus goes from one stop

to the next.

People can get on or off

at each stop.

In some buses, people can push a **button**.

That tells the **driver** to stop.

Buses help many people go to work or school.

button

Glossary

button

headlights

driver

route

Index

D
doors, 8

R
roads, 5

S
seats, 10

W
windows, 10